GOT?
Harmony!

Harmony
Lenoe

Quick Guide to Living Your Best Life!

By Lenise "Harmony" Halley

XULON PRESS

Xulon Press
2301 Lucien Way #415
Maitland, FL 32751
407.339.4217
www.xulonpress.com

ISBN-13: 978-1-6628-0250-8
Ebook: 978-1-6628-0251-5

Dedication

I dedicate this book to

My mom,
you left this world too young, but gave me every tool
you had to offer!

All of my children,
I hope that I have helped you to see life through a
healthier lens. It is the job of a parent to help their
children have a better experience than they had.
Mine has been great!

My family, friends, and clients,
you have heard all of these concepts too many
times over.
Thank you for reading it anyway.

My love,
thank you for being a part of this journey.

Table of Contents

Introduction:
Wait, What All Do You Do?

This is the question I am asked regularly. I now use my fingers to count my many professions and businesses. My normal response, "I am a Master Trainer, Group Exercise Instructor, Reiki Master Teacher, Arbonne Consultant, Life Coach, and I work for Fuller Theological Seminary in the Vocation and Formation department."

When people ask me how long I've been a coach, I usually say I don't know when it all started. I have always been an independent and responsible person, even as a young child. I took on responsibility with ease, and I was often the one people turned to for taking care of business. As the oldest of my siblings and most of my cousins, it was my responsibility to gather the troops and get the job done, even if it was just cleaning up the toys on the floor. It was my responsibility because it was a response to my ability. I did it well. If you ever meet my father, he is bound to tell you about how I had all his friends' kids marching and running drills in the grass while we were camping. I was a bossy kid, but I also could inspire people to do what we needed to do. From a young age, I learned to listen to people to find out what they wanted, develop a common ground, and get everyone to contribute towards that goal. I liked to win and liked the idea of winning together. So, I mastered the art of the win-win!

Along with this winning spirit, I always wanted to live well. I didn't have the words for this as a child, but I did realize that there were people in my family that I knew lived well. My grandparents were my first example because I spent every day with them after school. One Sunday morning, when I was five years old, I asked my grandmother if we were rich. Grandma Sugar stood on the church steps and said, "Yes, we are rich. But being rich is not measured by how much money you have, but rather the amount of love you have." This seed would grow in me throughout life. I believed my grandmother's words to be true because, to me, she seemed one of the most loving, kind-hearted people.

I knew my grandparents lived differently from the rest of our family. They appeared happily married. My grandfather was a pilot instructor after he retired from the post office. My grandmother worked for Community Support Services, an organization within the United Methodist church council. They were active, walked daily, bowled weekly, and went on vacations with our motorhome. It was not uncommon for my grandfather and I to go flying on a Saturday afternoon. We would jump in the car, drive to an airplane, fly around, and then go back home where grandma would have food waiting for us. This healthy, fun, and fulfilling lifestyle would result in them outliving all three of their children and a couple of their grandchildren, leaving me as their only surviving heir. As the only child left, I have spent the last ten years soaking up all of their wisdom.

Unfortunately, each of their children suffered from unhealthy habits like substance abuse, stress, and codependency. I am not sure what created the difference but, if I had to guess, I'd say it was my grandmother's intentional commitment to love, faith, and living a healthy life that sustained her. Their eldest child, my Auntie-Mommy (that is a combination of aunt and Godmother), knew that I would have to figure out how to avoid falling into the destructive patterns that she and her siblings had modeled. She started planting the seeds I could use to break these unhealthy behaviors early in my life. When I was eight years old, my Auntie-Mommy showed me how to meditate, started taking me to AL-Anon meetings, and taught me how to journal, say affirmations, and process my emotions. When I was a teenager, Auntie-Mommy sat me down and said it would be up to me to break the cycles of unhealthy codependent behavior that plagued her and her siblings. This conversation and many others continued to challenge me to be intentional about how I wanted to live.

Ultimately, my most significant discovery was learning how to love myself for who I am, where I am in my life's journey, and clearly defining my perfect self-expression. Once I found healthy self-love, the whole world opened up to me. I discovered how to live every day rich—rich in love, rich in spirit, rich in joy, and rich in peace. I start each day searching my soul for what I desire most and create plans to attract and achieve my goals. Along this journey, friends and family would ask to talk to me about their life—until one day, one of my best friends, Kat, sent me $40 after a conversation. She said I should not work for free. It was then that the idea of becoming a professional coach started to develop. I set my intention and prayed for God's guidance. As before, every step was laid out in front of me. The road was not always straight, but I learned to walk in faith and watch my life's work develop and grow. I was blessed beyond measure, and I found even more than I was looking for or could have imagined.

As a coach, I teach people how to love themselves, their families, and loved ones and how by doing so they can be in the right headspace to acquire all the things they want out of this life. This book is an introduction to the many ways I help people daily.

> *"Health, Wealth, Love, and Perfect Self-Expression.*
> *This is the square of life."*
> - Florence Shovel Shinn[1]

Chapter 1.
The Road to Self-Love

My greatest hope is that your love starts with you. It may be cliché to say, but if you do not love yourself first, you will have a hard time loving anyone else. Trying to love another person without self-love is like trying to fill a bucket with a hole in it. It's never enough. I intend to guide you through practices that can help mend the holes in your bucket so you can fill it up with love. We are going to call this patching up "self-work." Self-work seems so hard for so many of us because we would much rather focus on "fixing" everyone else but ourselves. When unhealthy codependency runs rampant it creates bitter, burnt-out people who blame everyone else for their poor health. Do you know someone who criticizes others but continues to sit in their own messy, unhappy life? I know them—I was one of them!

The idea that I had to take care of other people in order to be important or liked was a learned behavior. I often tell people more things are *caught* than *taught* to their children. My mom taught me early in life that I had to work twice as hard because I had two things working against me: being black and being a woman. She pushed me to work very hard and to be very self-disciplined. As a single mother, she too worked hard at everything she did. As I listened and watched, I learned her work ethic, dedication, and integrity. But I also caught her low self-esteem and poor self-image. I internalized the message that I had to work hard to win the love, admiration, and affection of others. I did not understand that being myself was enough for people to love.

I learned to wear the "competent and helpful friend" mask, the one who never left anyone hanging and could handle any task. I worked hard to prove I was worthy of friendship. If my friends needed me, I would deserve their love, right? Then I realized these same qualities enabled me to get ahead at work. I learned how to be a "go-to person." Being reliable became one of my winning strategies and ensured I was assigned all sorts of important things because I was smart, strong, and dependable. But I was rarely vulnerable, I didn't ask for space, time, or grace, and I never asked for help. I had learned to give help but did not know how to receive it.

I was always a human *doing* and had yet to learn how to be a human *being*. After a couple of years, this dynamic started to burn me out. I began to have this nagging feeling that people didn't like or respect me *for me*. I suspected they only wanted me around for what I could do and how I could serve *them* and *their* purpose. But who could blame them? I recognize now that I didn't show up as much more than a servant. I would hide how I felt to maintain the image of having it all together and appearing to be the perfect helper.

We live in a society where we are expected to put on a mask, and we learn early in life that we should show up a certain way. The world around us helps to mold and paint this mask.

"In this family, we…"

"As a woman, you need to carry yourself like this…"

"Boys only play with these kinds of toys…"

There are so many factors that color in these masks: race, culture, gender, our family of origin, hormones, sex. The list goes on. Once designed, the mask is strapped around our heads by the ego, and the ego's primary goals are to save face, look good, feel good, be right, and be the one in control. If we wear the mask long enough, we may form an unhealthy cognitive disconnection from where we end and the mask begins.

One of the remedies to this disconnection is self-reflection. When we are fully honest with ourselves, we realize sometimes we do not look good, we do not feel good, we are not right, and we are not in control. We sometimes let ourselves, and potentially others, down. To put it plainly, most of the time we are running around scared someone might figure out that we do not have it all together. **News Flash!** No one has it all together. I have seen, and even worn, the mask of the suffering servant and have learned that behind the mask the servant is usually suffering for attention and admiration. Even though they are suffering, they want to be admired for being the strong one who "takes care" of everyone. Even more so, they see themselves as the strong one who does not need anything and whom no one cares for in return.

I find two things, in particular, to be flawed when I hear people (even myself) describe themselves this way. First, when I ask if they have asked for help, interestingly (but not surprisingly) the majority of the time, the answer is NO. My follow-up question to this narrative is: why? Why did the suffering servant not let those around them know about their authentic experience? This question often takes some time to unpack because our egos work very hard to blame everyone else for our suffering instead of just claiming whatever fear is lurking within us. We look for what is most commonly accepted or avoid the fear of not being accepted. Deep down, we all just want to be loved and loveable. But to answer this question honestly, we have to accept ourselves in wholeness.

My journey to self-love is my gift called the present.

One of my favorite authors is Dr. Brené Brown. I love to hear her speak, and, even more so, I love to listen to her narrate her audiobooks. One of the reasons I connect with her writing is because she is an introvert like myself. It always takes people by surprise when I say that I am introverted because I am not shy, but the two traits are not mutually exclusive. I am very selective about the people I interact with because, while I love people, people drain me. Dr. Brené also writes as an empath, which I identify with as well. I naturally feel the emotions and energy of the people around me. I have had to learn how to both protect and clear other's energy in life, especially after any of my session's life coaching, training, performing Reiki, and even student calls. But most importantly, I connect with Dr. Brené because she made clear to me that by trying to win the love and admiration of my friends and family I was trying to "hustle for worthiness."[2] She has done *many* years of research on shame and written several books on how courage, fear, and vulnerability play crucial roles in our ability to establish deep connections with other people and live life *wholeheartedly*.

These lessons on wholehearted living helped me learn how to see myself as complete with my fears and how to navigate my vulnerability without working for my worth. I am a hard worker and it is part of who I am. But now, I no longer believe I have to work for others to love and cherish me. I work hard to make myself proud of who I am and who I want to be for myself. I have learned to see my strengths, weaknesses, achievements, mistakes, and everything in-between as a learning experience in my life's journey. And I am better for it. My ongoing effort in self-work has become my life's work, and I enjoy it every day. It is my gift to myself called the present.

The first step in self-work is learning to see yourself fully—you must take off the mask and accept what is underneath.

Exercise One: See Yourself!
Practice Self-Examination.

Here is your first assignment, *should you so choose to accept it*.

Play in the mirror!

Go to your favorite mirror, set a timer for three minutes, and leave it outside of your reach. Do not bring any distractions into the room with you (a bathroom is an excellent place for this exercise). Plant yourself in front of this mirror and look into your eyes. Do not do your makeup or shave; this is time for you to see yourself. Stay silent internally and externally. No words and no judgment, just look at yourself—eye to eye. When the timer goes off, the only words you will say are, "Thank you, I love you!" Repeat the exercise until it feels comfortable. Like any meditation, it may take a few tries before it feels right for you, but you are worth the effort.

Chapter 2.
Time to Dig Deep

I n every aspect of my career, I focus first on what is going on inside and usher clients to find the root of an issue or behavior. In fitness, I look first at how your body works, checking for any structural compensations the body has made to deal with imbalances. As a life coach, I dig into what someone wants most and what is holding them back. As a Reiki practitioner, I seek out where someone's energy is low or out of balance.

But when I first meet people, they are often asking me to "fix" something they are unhappy with externally. For example, when one of my infamous friends/clients, Gayl, hit me up on social media and asked me to "fix it," she meant the baby weight she had been carrying around two years after her son was born. When she started exercising with me, she had no clue how deep we would dig into her mind and body experience. Like many of us, she had not learned to make her inner life and well-being a priority. She was masking tons of internal pain, and this pain was created by the same traumas I had experiences as a child that turned into negative self-talk, depression, and poor self-care. For my friend, as with many of my clients, we worked on cleaning up the outside until she trusted me to help her clean up the inside. Now, she is enjoying life in a greater way.

I have found that many of my clients who are mothers (or parents in general) tend to put their internal health, both mental and physical, on the back burner. It is very common for my clients to be too busy to take a walk because they are taking their kids to their many obligations like school, dance class, or sports practice. Then spend the bulk of their time figuring out quick and easy food to make for dinner while helping with homework, washing clothes, and cleaning up around the house. Most of them come to me first as personal training clients because they see that their bodies don't look the same. I often ask questions that seem weird to them, like when was the last time you took some time to meditate, relax, give yourself a pamper day, read a good book, or do some journaling. This is usually laughed at or met with a blank stare because they can't remember. Then I usually ask, "When did you decide your child's happiness was a replacement for your own?"

This is a question that was developed over time. It is not always a conscious decision, and I do understand there is happiness gained by watching our children experience life's pleasures. But when did we decide that we didn't need to make time for our own pleasure or even self-care? There are a variety of internal narratives that support this messaging, and I am not saying that it is totally wrong or bad. I always ask my clients if their lifestyle is working for them and, if not, may I help them discover other ways of living that might be supportive and fulfilling.

Be kind to yourself—you teach people how to treat you by example.

In addition to our children, we sometimes focus on our career as a distraction from internal pain. One day, a client shared a story with me about his friend whom he considered very successful. She has a great job, makes great money, and is great with her kids. However, this same friend is also unhealthy, has unresolved trauma, and is mentally stuck in a rut. I'm always curious to see how people view success. Is success an amount of money or a job title? Money can't buy self-worth, self-esteem, peace, or joy, but it's much easier to mask what's going on inside when you are validated by what's going on outside. Material things can distract us temporarily, but ultimately the darkness buried will always resurface.

Anyone who has been on a trip with someone they didn't like—whether it's a sibling on a road trip or an annoying person sitting beside you on a long plane ride—understands that if you are going to spend a lot of time with a person, you might want to enjoy their company. Otherwise, it's going to be rough! Well, the same is true for you and yourself. You are going to spend more time with yourself than anyone else in this lifetime. The sooner you get right with you, the easier it is to deal with life. Life is a game, not a battle, so help yourself get to know, support, and love "Team YOU."

You might be asking yourself, what does it look like when you are "right within"? If you are unfamiliar with what that means, you should listen to "Doo Wop" by Lauryn Hill, who spells it out in a few lines so beautifully:

> *Girlfriend, let me break it down for you again*
> *You know I only say it 'cause I'm truly genuine*
> *Don't be a hard rock when you really are a gem[3]*

Do you treat yourself like you are a hard rock or a gem? Do you expect everything to be difficult? Do you act like you can handle a beating? Maybe you can, and I'm not saying you can't, but is that what you want and deserve?

Now, let me clarify a little. I'm not opposed to being strong. Nor am I demeaning a hard workout. Nor am I debating whether one should box like a boss and show toughness and strength. I am talking about how you genuinely treat yourself *within*. What are your internal conversations like? How do you care for yourself? Some of the strongest people on earth have the best self-care habits. They treat themselves well. This goes for men, women, and all identities in-between. However, you experience your gender or sexuality does not mean you need to treat yourself harshly.

How do we treat gems? With respect and reverence. We take our time when looking at them, we inspect them, we see their differences as beautiful and love to see them sparkle. If you are anything like me, you might have beautiful rocks and crystals. You may spend time researching their qualities and clean, clear, and charge them to replenish their energy. In much the same way, our inner beauty is worth being cleared, charged, and reflected upon to set ourselves up as the precious jewels that we are in our own lives.

Exercise Two: Meditation

I believe that you should get real with who you are this very moment. This can take 5 minutes or 50 minutes, however long you can stand it. Sit in quiet, without distractions, and check-in with yourself. Start by paying attention to your heartbeat. Next, listen to the rhythm of your breathing. Then, move into examining what's on your mind. What are you thinking about? Is it worth your time? Engage your imagination: try to visualize each thought rising to the sky and floating away with the clouds. After you have thought all of the thoughts and have sat with yourself as long as you can stand it, give yourself a big hug. The only words you will speak when you are finished are, "Thank you, I love you!"

Visualization

Imagine yourself as that beautiful gem. It is your birthright to shine! What kind of a gem are you? If you cannot identify with one right away, look up your birthstone. How has your life polished you already, with all the living you have already done, in the rock tumbler of life? What are your colors? What are your facets? What are your imperfections? How and where can you best shine?

This practice of sitting with yourself is the beginning of any kind of change and growth. Take it easy on yourself, you are a precious gem worthy of care.

"The unexamined life is not worth living."
- Socrates[4]

Chapter 3.
But *Why?*

There is a pivotal point in each of our lives around the age of two or three when we ask the question "why." I was nine years old when my little brother went through his "why" stage, and he almost drove me to lose my mind. He had more questions than any of us had answers. Even today, he still has more questions than I have answers for, but now I tell him to ask Google. I can't be too mad at my brother, though. According to my father, I have been asking people "why" for as long as he can remember. My father went on to say that I made him understand that "why" was the most powerful word in the English language. I still drive most people crazy with questions, but they tolerate "why" because "why" is significant and challenging.

As children we ask "why" because we are trying to understand the world around us, but as we get older we can forget to continue asking these questions. When we dig into our "why" we find that many things we believe are true were *caught* rather than *taught*. There is an old story of a young girl who is learning to cook a ham. As the young girl watched her mother cook, she noticed her mom cut the ends off the ham. Curious, she asked her mom why she did that, and the mom replied, "I don't know, that's how your grandmother always did it." The young girl reached out to ask her grandmother why she cut the ends off the ham, to which the grandmother replied, "That is the only way it would fit in my baking pan."

This story is an excellent example of how we "catch" so many of our beliefs from the decisions of the people around us. This is the reason I continue asking "why" as I dig down into the roots of my clients' Thoughts, Beliefs, and Decisions (TBD). Conventionally speaking, TBD means "to be determined." I believe both meanings equally apply because your Thoughts, Beliefs, and Decisions will *determine* how your life progresses. What we believe shapes our reality. But sometimes we need help navigating the parts of ourselves that make us uncomfortable.

Digging into our TBDs is challenging and many will cut themselves short by answering "why" with "I don't know." But if we don't know ourselves, we limit ourselves. My most significant source of personal accountability comes from continuously teaching this concept. I must work on my thought-life every day. I have to exercise, eat healthily, read, pray, say my affirmations, and listen to the wisdom teachers who help to feed my soul to keep myself mentally healthy. I reflect on how I am showing up for myself, my clients, family, and friends. I search my soul for what I need and ask for help when I need it. I reflect on my rituals to see what is working and what needs to be changed. It is a practice I have learned to make my priority. My "why" is simple: it brings me joy.

Exercise Three: Examine Your "Why"

Take a look at your everyday life. We brush our teeth the way our parents taught us as a kid. Our wake-up routine is likely the same since high school or the military. We raise our children the way we were raised. We keep on keeping on the way we always have because we feel like it's worked for us this long. But do we know the "why" behind it?

Self-Reflection Without Judgment

Reflect on your daily routine without weighing whether it is good or bad, justified or unjustified. Instead, the best measurement should be if it still serves your greatest good.

Get Curious

What do you like to do?
Where do you like to go?
How do you want to live?
What do you think about how you look?
What do you say about how you look?
What impact do you want to leave on the world?

Chapter 4.
Create Your New Normal

I always start my life coaching by diving into my clients' mental environment because that is the place you inevitably spend the most time. You can reimagine the inner environment you navigate life with over and over again until you create the life you want to live. Like Dr. Wayne Dyer said "When you change how you look at things, what you are looking at changes".[5] I learned this practice from my grandmother long before the world-renowned book *The Secret* introduced the law of attraction. I spent a lot of time with my grandmother throughout my life, and she has always been one of the most positive people I have ever met.

Good habits can be formed to dissolve old habits if the habit no longer suits the person. We can work diligently to focus on what we want, acknowledge what we dislike, and continue to grow. The old saying goes "it's hard to teach old dogs new tricks," but hard does not mean impossible. With advancements in neuroscience, especially within the concept of neuroplasticity, we have learned that when old dogs learn new tricks it helps ward off diseases like dementia and relieves PTSD, depression, and anxiety. Neuroplasticity describes how neural pathways are developed, hardened, and dissolved in your brain. This is basically how our thoughts and behaviors are formed and solidified over time and practice.

Let's make it simple, shall we? Like ABC.

What you believe to be true is valid until you are convinced otherwise. Your whole life lives in your mind, and within your mind there are various levels of consciousness. For this chapter, I will only discuss two: your conscious mind and subconscious mind. Your conscious mind is where you acknowledge your thoughts, or the forefront of your mind. If compared to your favorite song, this is where your lyrics live. Your subconscious is what's on your mind without being aware that you are thinking about it. It keeps on going even if it is not your major focal point. Your subconscious is where the beat and melody live, and you are rocking and popping to it all day long.

I learned early in life that there were three children's songs that use the same melody—the "Alphabet" song, "Twinkle, Twinkle, Little Star," and "Baa, Baa, Black Sheep." Much like these songs, you can keep the same melody and change your lyrics to create a new experience. If you realize from doing the previous exercises that you have been singing a sad or damaging song about your life, maybe it's time for a remix. You can start by getting back to your ABCs to write some new lyrics to live by: A is for Affirmations, B is for Believe, and C is for Change.

Affirmations

One definition of the word *affirmation is* "something affirmed: a positive assertion."[6] Affirmations are traditionally short positive statements that you can repeat easily. They may rhyme or have a rhythm to them, but they do not *have* to be short and they do not *have* to rhyme. I find that affirmations are most impactful when they are written in the present tense, positive, and frequently used. I like to use "I am," "I will," and "My perfect" statements.

I am loved, lovable, and surrounded by loving energy.

I did not always feel loved or loveable or surrounded by loving energy, but I do now.

I will pass this test and move on to be a great Personal Trainer.

I did not pass it the first time, but I did the second time and went on to be a great personal trainer.

My perfect self-expression is manifesting every day.

Though this wasn't always true for me, I now wake up every day feeling loved, successful, and fulfilled—even on the days it is hardest to get out of bed.

I see my life becoming more beautiful in every way. I have goals and continue to work on making my life better, so my affirmations are always working.

Another great example of an affirmation is the "Five Reiki Principles":

Just for today, I will not worry
Just for today, I will not be angry
Just for today, I will work honestly and with integrity
Just for today, I be grateful for my many blessings
Just for today, I will be kind to every living thing[7]

I have a curtain in my home that reads:

I am a being of light and love
I am infinite and boundless
I am divinely guided and inspired
I embody my spiritual gifts
I embrace the unity of all beings
I am one with all of creation[8]

Believe

You believe the stories and thoughts that you tell yourself. You especially believe your voice more than any other noise. I believe that this is the reason people recite scriptures often. They want to remind themselves of the promises of God. We start using affirmations to remind ourselves to think positively about our lives, even if we do not believe it at that moment. The idea is to continue to say your affirmations until you train your brain to believe the words that you say.

One of the affirmations that I created for myself is, "I am an amazing coach and trainer; I coach and train people all day, every day." When I started this was not the case, but it is now. Once I started practicing Reiki, I created a new affirmation: "I am a blessed Master Trainer, Coach, and Reiki Master Teacher. I bless people, and they find value in this combination of services." When I started practicing Reiki I was not a Master Teacher, but I am now. I kept saying it until I believed it, and it became true.

Change

I cannot stress this point enough: we learn by repetition. There are so many timeless truths that teach about practice and repetition. For those parents and teachers out there, you know anything that you are teaching you have to repeat over and over again. Athletes, dancers, singers, and creative people all know that anything that you want to get better at, you have to practice. It's not just practice that makes perfect—*perfect* practice makes perfect. The reason for this goes back to neuroplasticity. When you are trying to relearn things, you need to make sure you are creating new neural pathways to combat the old ways of thinking that you have built up over time. Once new neural pathways are created, they take repetition to harden.

I explain it like this: have you ever rearranged your room? The first night when you wake up to go to the bathroom, you will probably try to turn the light on the same way you did before the room was rearranged. You might even run into a few things along the way. This is because the old way of navigating your space has been stored in your subconscious and muscle memory. You did not have to think about it because you had repeated the actions for so long. After you rearrange your room, you have to relearn your midnight route to the bathroom. Over time you learn your new route because, day after day, you take the same steps. It becomes natural. The same is true for retraining your way of thinking about and navigating your life.

Exercise Four: Create Your New ABCs

Step 1: *Develop a new idea that you want to believe to be true.*

Step 2: *Create your affirmation.*

Step 3: *Write it down where you can see it.*

I have gone as far as writing a note and posting it on the medicine cabinet and sending it via text message to myself.

Step 4: *Repeat, Repeat, Repeat.*

Repeat your affirmation and believe it ***as much as you possibly can***. I refer to people's ability often because I believe we should always embrace just how much we are capable of doing. Sometimes things are hard, but hard is still possible. During my mother's battle with multiple sclerosis, I watched her body waste away slowly. She gradually lost her ability to walk, sit up, talk, chew, and swallow until her heart finally gave up.

So, my philosophy is to always use your ability to the fullest and "Do it because you can!"

Step 5: *Use your creativity to repeat your affirmation.*

Sing the affirmation to yourself. Write it down and read it to yourself. Recite it and believe it to be your act of affirming yourself. Believe it to be a solemn declaration made under penalty of perjury because you have taken an oath to believe it. Practice, repeat, sing it, rap it—practice, repeat. Continue to repeat until it is natural, and if your old habits or thought patterns return, practice over and over again. Repeat, repeat, repeat!

We can learn our ABCs over again: Affirmations, Believe, and Change.

Chapter 5.
Move Your Body

Now that we have spent some time getting your head in the game, let's dig into your physical health. Much like the word "success," I find the meaning of the terms "health" and "healthy" have much to do with each persons' perspective and may have many influences—biological, cultural, personal preference, etc. In this book, I am going to talk about two areas of health: fitness and fuel.

Fitness–How Your Body Moves and Performs

We will start with fitness solely because a wise client once told me, "If exercise were a pill, it would be the cure for everything!" I believe our bodies were made to move because when they don't our health and quality of life suffer.

When your friends and family know you are a trainer, it's a topic that usually comes up at parties and family functions. *It also means I end up in way too many push up challenges, at a moment's notice. Last birthday party I went to I did 200 push-ups before I left.* Back to my point, once people hear I am a trainer or a coach they have questions. Everyone wants to know two things: what can I do to get rid of "this" and build up "that" (usually, the "this" is a fat deposit, and the "that" is muscle). Every time, I respond the same way: "It all depends on your body and how it performs." You have to understand that everything about your body is there for a reason, whether you are very physically fit, overweight, have had an injury or two, or even had a kid or two. No judgment, things are what they are.

So, what we have to do first is understand how your body loads and uses what it has to offer. Every trainer worth their certification performs fitness assessments and, as a Master Trainer, I have performed countless. A trainer may have you go through an overhead squat assessment, gait assessment, Landing Error Scoring Screening (LESS), or they may just watch you stand and walk around. Many things are understood by learning how each body moves.

Exercise Five: Basic Exercise Assessment and Workout

For the sake of this book, I will give you one way to observe how your body functions by using a sample fitness test. But there are a couple pieces of advice to consider before jumping in. Your ability to perform each exercise safely should be your top priority at all times. First, you should always consult your doctor before starting a new exercise routine, especially if you have any underlying health concerns. Second, you are not trained on exactly what to look for, but you can watch yourself for safety awareness by looking in a mirror or recording yourself. I have taught all of my clients that Rule Number One is "Don't Die!" Rule Number One can be extended to mean: breathe, hydrate, stretch, slow down between reps so you do not injure yourself, and anything else that prioritizes your health and safety while you exercise.

Basic Exercise Assessment

I recommend warming up before exercising. This can be as light as a 15-minute walk or as exciting as a five-minute high-intensity interval training warm up. Start where you are most comfortable. If you are new to exercising or have not exercised in the last two months you should consider yourself a beginner. If you are a former athlete but have been out of training for a few weeks, start off as a beginner as well.

For the basic assessment, count how many of each of the following exercises you can do in one minute. You can use your basic assessment number as a way to build out your exercise plan and as a way to keep moving. Most of my clients start by using this assessment as homework. They do three sets of the basics on their days in between their scheduled workout sessions.

You can also use this basic assessment as a measure to gauge consistency and progress. Keep note of how many reps you can do at the start of each month. Does your number of reps go up, down, or stay the same? Remember: do not perform any of these exercises if they are painful or if your doctor has advised against them. Modify any of these exercises if **you are not able to perform them with good form.**[1] If you

---

[1] Note: Good form is always the key to success when it comes to exercising because you want to be sure to reduce the likelihood of injury.

are unsure of what good form is or need help getting started, you may reach out for a fitness consultation. https://gotharmony.org/master-trainer/

_____ Basic crunch
_____ Push-ups _____ Back extension
_____ Hip raises

This exercise is for more advanced performance.[2] Time how long you can hold a plank in good form.

_____ Plank

---

[2] Advance performance means that you already workout regularly (two to three times per week), are aware of good form, and/or workout with a coach or trainer who can monitor your performance to reduce the likelihood of injury.

3-Day Workout Plan for Beginners to Advanced

Did you say you wanted a good work out? Well, here you go! The following are two basic three-day workout plans. Use the same safety advice as above and consult your doctor before starting. Watch or record yourself, and **do not continue to do anything that is painful**. And always remember Rule Number One: Don't Die!

Some terms might seem unfamiliar because there are many different names for some exercises. For example, I have heard a hip bridge called a floor bridge, hip lifts, and hip bridges all in the same day while walking around the gym. If you need any pointers or clarifications, you are welcome to reach out for a fitness consultation.

Beginners

Day One		
Warm-up	**Core**	**Upper Body**
(Timed 30 second intervals)	(10 reps each exercise, 3 sets)	(10 reps each exercise, 3 sets. Use resistance bands or weights.)
Jog	Basic crunches	Bicep curls
Jumping jacks	Hip bridges	Overhead press
High knees (march in place)	Alternating leg lifts (10 each side)	Front raise
Butt kicks	Push-ups	Side raise
	Mountain climbers	Triceps extension
Day Two		
Warm-up	**Core**	**Lower Body**
(Timed 30 second intervals)	(10 reps each exercise, 3 sets)	(10 reps each exercise, 3 sets)
Jog	Basic crunches	Standard squats
Jumping jacks	Hip bridges	Backward stepping lunges
High knees	Alternating leg lifts (10 each side)	Forward stepping lunges
Butt kicks	30-second plank	Side stepping lunges
	Bird dog (10 each side)	Calf raises

Day Three		
Warm-up	**Core**	**Pyramid**
(Timed 30 second intervals)	(10 reps each exercise, 3 sets)	(Start with 1 rep, then increase each set by 1 until reaching 5 reps, then go back by 1 rep each set)
Jog	Elbows to knees, fingers to toes	Walkout
Side lunges	Squats	push-up
Squats	Hip circles	Mountain climber
High knees	Side lunges (isolate both sides)	
Butt kicks	Alternating reverse lunges	

Intermediate to Advanced

Day One		
Warm-up	**Core**	**Work**
(Timed 30 second intervals)	(10-15 reps each exercise, 3 sets)	(10-15 reps each exercise, 3 sets)
Jog	Russian twists (10 each side)	Jump squats (12 reps)
Side lunges	Boat crunches	Split jumps (20 seconds)
Squats	V ups	Forward/backward bounding (10 reps)
High knees	Bird dog (10 each side)	Side lunge w/touch down (20 reps)
Butt kicks	Plank 2 push-ups (10 each side)	Reverse lunge (20 reps)
Quick feet wide	Mountain climbers (10 each side)	Around the world lunges
Quick feet narrow	Plank jacks	(3 positions, 10 each side)
	Plank (1 minute)	

Day Two		
Warm-up	**Core**	**Pyramids 1-7-1**
(Timed 30 second intervals)	(10 reps each exercise, 3 sets)	(Start with 1 rep, then increase each set by 1 until reaching 7 reps, then go back by 1 rep each set)
Jog	Elbows to knees fingers to toes	
Side lunges	Squats	Walkout push up-shoulder tap
Squats	Hip circles	Mountain climber
High knees	Side lunges (isolate both sides)	Plank jack
Butt kicks	Reverse lunges alternate	
Squat jumps		
Squat kick		
Day Three		
Warm-up	**Core**	**Stretch**
(Timed 30 second intervals)	(16 reps each exercise, 5 Sets)	(Hold each pose for 20-30 seconds)
Jog	Jumping jacks	Child's pose
Jumping jacks	Squats	Cat to Cow
High knees	Sit-ups	Runner's lunge
Butt kicks	Push-ups	Pigeon
Standing hip circles	Burpees	

Chapter 6. Food is Fuel

As a trainer, people ask me what they should eat. I remain in my scope of practice, but I have learned to ask a lot of questions. Your relationship with food is not just about what you eat. It's everything from when you eat, how much, how often, who you eat with, where you eat, and why you eat. Don't forget how quickly and late you eat. All these questions will help you examine some of the Who, What, When, Where, Why, and How of your nutrition.

I have taught many people how to monitor their macro-nutrition (or macros), which is a way of looking at your diet based on the dominant type of nutrition you are receiving from your food. People usually assess their macros by looking at the percentage of protein, carbohydrates, and fats they are taking in. For example, you'll often hear people describe their diet primarily by the way they acquire protein. In my experience, they'll usually first tell me whether they eat meat, fish only, no meat, or some variation like, "I only eat chicken and turkey." Then they'll normally point out if they eat based on a specific program like paleo, keto, or the South Beach Diet®. These programs outline strict ways of eating macronutrients. A very important point to understand about macro-nutrition is that the foods we eat rarely fit into only one category; many foods offer protein, carbohydrates, and fats. For example, legumes provide all three of the macronutrients. Everyone's body is different and your ability to obtain nutrients from different foods may vary.

Many people find value in keeping a food journal. In one of my disciplines, I have learned to journal what I eat and how it makes my body feel by listing out different foods as Red, Yellow, and Green. Red foods are things I do not eat or that do not agree with my body (like dairy). Yellow foods are things that I can eat but are not the most optimal foods for my body to run on (like chocolate chip cookies). Green foods are lean proteins, leafy greens, and healthy fiber and fats (like chicken, kale, celery, apples, and hummus).

I have learned to ask people to define their own goals with food and what they would like to achieve.

For this book, I'm sticking to the same concept of examining the thoughts around our actions because I have found that many people already know what they need to do. Information is literally at our fingertips all day long with our smartphones. What most people need help with is getting real with themselves on what they are doing. But to start, there are a few fundamental truths that might help you. First off, there is an energy flow with food. Following the basic rule of thermodynamics, if you take in more calories (or energy) than you use or exert, you will gain weight. If you take in less than you use or exert, you lose weight. If your intake and output are the same, you tend to stay the same. There are minimal exceptions to these rules. Secondly, treat your body well by fueling it with high-quality nutrition. You will get out of it what you put into it.

Eating healthy may mean you'll need to negotiate your budget to make sure you are improving the quality of your food. Believe me, whether or not you decide to invest in your nutrition, you are going to pay for it one way or another. Some people wished they had made their health a priority before they were given strict doctor's orders and prescriptions. It takes time, energy, and resources to make sure you are eating nutrient-rich food. My own desire to guide people to high-quality food for fuel resulted in the divine connection that exposed me to a green, clean, vegan, wellness company that I immediately invested in and continue to share daily. This company revealed products that help to overhaul my body from what I clean my skin with to how clean I keep myself running.

If we want to keep our energy up, we have to make sure we are using high-quality fuel.

The following is my personal food plan that you can use as inspiration toward creating your own. My father taught me early, "If you fail to plan then you plan to fail." I have been working on my food plan for years now, and I do the best when I plan a head. Keep in mind, I am not a nutritionist, nor do I give complete dietary advice. While I have Precision Nutrition certification in Exercise Nutrition, I am simply sharing what works for me.

What – The Five-Fingers of Food:

Thumb–water
Pointer finger–fruit
Middle finger–vegetables
Ring finger–meat or other proteins like beans
Pinkie–nuts/avocados or other healthy fats

Why:

Thumb–Water: Water gets the thumbs up because I work hard to get 64+ ounces of water a day. Everyone who knows me knows my 64-ounce water jug is always with me.

Pointer Finger–Fruit: Fruit takes the first finger because it's great in the morning when I need the sugar and have time to burn it off. I reduce the amount of simple carbohydrates (like fruit) I eat after lunch.

Middle Finger–Vegetables: Veggies are the middle finger because it's my longest finger. It is the largest portion on every plate, and I strive to make 51% of my diet raw fruits and veggies, including one green salad per day. I have started my own garden, where I grow non-GMO vegetables. I try to make my vegetable intake colorful by enjoying various shades of cabbage and kale together with bright bursts of bell peppers and herbs.

Ring Finger–Meat (or beans): Meat is the ring finger because it's a life source, as the only finger that has a vein that runs to my heart. This also includes all other sources of protein like legumes and nuts. I eat protein all day because we do not store much of it in our body even though we use it for energy. Protein also helps us feel full longer.

Pinkie Finger–Healthy Fats: Pinkie finger is for healthy fats because I should only have small portions as a snack or as my favorite hummus in my salad. I also eat trail mix, raw nuts, and nut butters. An apple with almond butter is one of my favorite morning snacks (you can also swap the apple for celery for an afternoon snack). Remember, foods offer a variety of macronutrients. Many of the foods I have listed for healthy fats also may turn into carbohydrates and some even have protein.

When:

- Drink 16oz of water AS SOON AS I WAKE UP.
- Drink water all day by carrying a 64-ounce water jug everywhere. (It's heavy when it is full, so I am encouraged to drink it to lighten the load.)
- Eat something every 3-4 hours.
- Stop eating solid foods at 7:30 pm.

How:

- I eat 5-6 small meals the size of my fist.
- If I eat out, I immediately cut the serving portions in half and place the second half away so I do not overeat.
- I eat until I have finished my portion, then I drink water to allow myself time to feel full or satisfied.
- I do not eat until I feel stuffed.

Who:

You and your family, friends, and loved ones all benefit from you exploring what foods work best to fuel your life. You may need to spend some time to find out what foods fit in your schedule. Take time to explore your diet with yourself and those around you. Our "who" can also include outside help like an Exercise Nutrition Coach. When my doctor told me I was prediabetic, I knew my life needed to change. I started exercising more and collaborated with friends to try out new ways of eating. We even shared meals and recipes. In time I realized that, while I really enjoyed that dynamic, I needed more of a push. So, I reached out a Personal Trainer who is now one of my closest friends, Latina. I asked her to train me as well as to help me become a great trainer. She taught me some great lessons that I put to use once I earned my own Personal Training Certification.

Most importantly, I learned to own my story and share it with others so that they know I understand how challenging it can be to make these changes but to continue saying, "It is hard but well worth it." Now, I help people explore what works for them and how to stay accountable to their nutrition goals. But to be clear, the ultimate Who is always you! It is up to you to make your nutrition a priority and do what you need to care for yourself. There is no shame if this includes seeking professional help whether from a coach or doctor.

Exercise Six: You Are What You Eat, So Who Are You?

(Remember: no judgment)

I challenge you to examine your day and how you are feeding your life. Look into the Who, What, When, Where, Why, and How behind your eating.

What feeds your body, mind, and soul?

What feeds your brain?

Who do you eat with most often? How do your values align?

What does your eating plan look like? Do you have a plan?

When do you eat?

Where do you eat most often?

Why do you eat?

How do you eat?

What types of foods are you eating?

How are you preparing your food?

How efficiently and effectively is your digestive system using what you are taking in?

How often are you eating?

How much are you consuming in your portions?

Chapter 7.
Money is Currency

Another topic I am often asked about is money. Through many years of helping people create budgets and clean up their credit, I learned there is little lasting impact when you help someone without addressing their relationship with money. Our money habits are often also caught and taught from childhood without ever questioning our beliefs as we grow older. So, let's first dig into what money actually is.

Money is currency. We understand this when we travel outside the country because we exchange our local currency to the currency of the place we'll be traveling. But, while money is one type of currency, it is not the only form. So, what is currency?

Currency: circulation as a medium of exchange[9]

We exchange our time for money when we work. We exchange our money for goods when we go shopping. But looking at the course of human history, we know that many forms of currency existed before money. People used to trade other things of value—grain for silver, animals for bread, spices for fabric, and so on. Love is also a currency. You will do things for people you love for little to nothing in return because it is a circulation and exchange.

The word currency shares a root with the word current, which is all about movement. Like energy, currency must move. Money must also circulate and move. We understand on a fundamental level that money moves and exchanges hands all day every day. This is not bad or harmful.

What I commonly found in my coaching is that many of us have fear related to money. Some of us were raised with a scarcity mindset about currency (or money) where we learned to believe there was never enough or we were going to run out of it. This fear perpetuates itself in navigating life and wealth of all kinds. When we feel like there is never enough, we have to hold on to what we have or hurry up and spend it before it is taken. We may buy a bunch of things to make us feel better or show off our financial status. We might dress a certain way or drive a certain car to prove to others that we have money. There is nothing wrong with spending money on what you like if you can afford it. The problem is usually created when we are spending from fear—fear of acceptance, fear of pity, fear of unworthiness.

I have many clients whose fear of lack or scarcity mindset leads them to buy things that they never use and end up in storage. I am not a big fan of stashing things in storage units for long periods of time because, from my own experience working at a storage facility, I know customers rarely visit, default on their payments, and end up with their stuff auctioned off. Many of my clients spend hundreds of dollars every month storing things that they do not use. Some have even replaced items that are in storage with newer versions of the same things because they forgot that they already had it or did not want to take the time to find it.

When I look at people's finances to see how much money they are spending on storing things they are not using, I try to explain how the stagnation of holding on to things that are not being used can hold them back. I try to help show them how much of their budget, time, and mental space they can free up by just letting go. Allowing the things that are held up in storage to be sold or donated often gives them more resources to move forward. I also explain that by re-appropriating the money they were spending on a storage unit, they can grow their wealth through savings and investing. I usually throw in one of my favorite sayings, "It is very hard to pick up new things when your hands are full with old things."

I learned this lesson when my first Godson Andrew was a baby. He wanted whatever toy I picked up. So, when he would crawl over to me I would ask him for the toy he already had. Puzzled, he would look at me like, "Why can't I have it all?" Even if he didn't give me the other toy, he would always put whatever he was playing with down. Sometimes we have to look at what we are holding on to that no longer serves our highest good.

The truth is that having "things" usually makes people feel more secure. Their mind is holding onto a time when they did not have enough or they were scared they were not going to have enough. So, they now want to feel like they have *more* than enough. What you believe about how currency flows through your life is what you experience. As I quoted before, if you change how you look at things, what you're looking at changes.[10] Even if you are today years old the first time you are learning this lesson, it is not too late to change your beliefs. You have the power to learn new thought processes and skills to change your relationship with currency. Checking in with your TBDs (Thoughts, Beliefs, and Decisions) around money will help you work through any fears and negative patterns that no longer serve you.

Exercise Seven: Currency Exploration

Step 1: Examine Your Thoughts About Currency

(Remember: no judgment)

How do you feel about currency?
What is your relationship with currency?
How do you want to feel about currency?
What do you want to learn about currency?

Step 2. See Yourself

Look in the mirror and remind yourself, "I have more than enough, and I am more than enough."

Step 3. Meditate

Take a moment to meditate on how you are treating yourself. Are you treating yourself like you lack something or are making up for lost time? Are you holding on to things even though you have a deep-seated feeling it is time to let them go?

Step 4. Examine Your "Why?"

Your "why" around money might sound something like, "I used to feel like my mom and I never had enough money, and that fear of lack has guided my decisions. My family may have struggled growing up, but I have much more financial freedom now."

Step 5. Create New ABCs:

Choose an **affirmation** that calls currency to flow freely through your life. For example, "Rhythm, harmony, and balance are now established in my mind, body and affairs."[11] Repeat your affirmation all day every day until you **believe** it. Remember, **change** takes time, practice, and repetition. But anything worth having is worth working for, and you are worth it.

Chapter 8.
Perfect Self-Expression

Discovering your perfect self-expression is finding a way to live your life out loud as a dedication to yourself. It is a way to give your life the meaning that your soul desires. Some may describe it as finding your vocation or the existential meaning to your life's journey. This is a quest each of us must search our souls to define. Some find this meaning through exercises like writing a personal mission or vision statement or even writing an obituary as a practice to define what we want to have accomplished before our body leaves this earth.

To find my perfect self-expression, I spent many years developing who I am and who I want to look at in the mirror. I asked myself the same questions I have asked you in the preceding pages, and I continue to ask myself them regularly. I tried various careers and lifestyles to find what fit. I ended up a trainer because I asked myself, "Where is the one place I would never tire of being?" And my answer was the gym. I learned that I longed to workout while I was training my clients, so I became a fitness instructor. I became a coach after many years of looking into a variety of psychology and coaching programs and discovering that I was drawn to the progression of the coaching models. In all aspects of my career, I tried different options until I found what I continuously enjoyed and best served my life.

I started practicing Reiki, which is a relaxation and energy healing technique, after I was diagnosed with a condition that plagues more than 50% of black women that is rarely discussed: fibroids. Fibroids can be painless and symptom-free or cause excessive bleeding and tons of pain. Mine was the latter. One day during meditation, I had the idea to learn how to heal myself. And true to form, every avenue opened up for me.

My Reiki practice did not exactly remove my fibroids, but it helped heal the anxiety and mental anguish I was dealing with daily. It is a practice used for deep relaxation and channeling light energy throughout the body, so it is very soothing. While searching for treatment, I went to a doctor who gave me the scare of a lifetime by suggesting that a partial or complete hysterectomy was my best viable treatment course. Thankfully, through prayer, meditation, Reiki, and the tenacity not to give up, I found another practitioner who offered a minimally invasive treatment. My recovery was flawless. I currently have no scars, pain, or discomfort. I also have full functionality of my reproductive organs. Now, I offer Reiki treatments and teach Reiki to others as a way to relieve stress and relax. The best part is that when I give a Reiki treatment, I get a Reiki treatment. Everyone wins. I cannot stress this point enough—everyone benefits from you creating the healthiest version of yourself.

I share these experiences as examples of my will to create what I had never seen but believed could be true. Many people put off the need for personal development and self-care work, but you have already started this journey so I know you are ready to explore the possibilities of fulfilling your deepest dreams. Ask yourself the following questions to find what brings you closer to your perfect self-expression. As always, be honest and open with no judgment.

Exercise Eight: What Are Your Deepest Desires?

Step 1. Self-Reflection

What is your deepest dream for your life?

Is there a need that you see in the world that only you can fill?

Do you believe in yourself and your plan to make a mark on this world?

What do you want your life's work to be?

Step 2. See Yourself

Look in the mirror and remind yourself, "I have more than enough and I am more than enough." Strike your favorite superhero pose. My favorite pose is having my hands on my hips, chest lifted with my shoulders rounded back and down, and my head held high!

Step 3. Meditate:

Take a moment to meditate on how you are treating yourself. Are you holding yourself back? Are you playing small? Are you doing what you love to do, whether it is a hobby, side job, volunteer work, or your main work? Are you free to be who you want to be?

Step 4. Examine Your Why?

Finding your "why" around your deepest desires may start with asking yourself something like, "Why did I decide my dreams were less important or impossible?"

Step 5. Create New ABCs:

Choose an ***affirmation*** that calls in your deepest desires. For example, "I am harmonious, happy and divinely magnetic, and now draw to me my ships over a calm sea."[12] Repeat this affirmation all day every day until you ***believe*** it. ***Change*** takes time, practice, and repetition, but you are worth the effort it takes to explore the dreams that are hidden in the depths of your soul.

Chapter 9.
The 2020 Global Pandemic

The fact that we are all living in a global pandemic is not lost on me or on the challenges that I am addressing in the book. I am well aware that many people lost their life savings when their businesses closed, lost loved ones to COVID-19, or are navigating how to make a living while helping their children with distance learning. Here in sunny California, we lived through triple digit weather and months-long wildfires that cost many people their homes and covered surrounding cities with ash and smoke. Since the start of the pandemic, Los Angeles County has maintained a high number of COVID-19 cases, especially for the state of California, forcing many businesses to stay closed or reinvent how they operate altogether. The gym where I previously spent most of my day has been closed since March, with the exception of a couple weeks in late June before it closed again mid-July. Even with all of the precautions being taken, it is uncertain whether larger gyms will ever get back to the way things were.

We have been hearing people talk about how face masks and social distancing are the new normal. Others are patiently awaiting a vaccine in hopes that we can slow the spread of this silent killer. I have lost family members and loved ones. I have known friends who caught the virus as frontline essential workers, recovered, and went back out to work on the frontlines again. I know people who have tested positive with little to no symptoms. I have a client who is the mother of seven children in elementary school through high school who had to quit her job to make sure all of her kids are focusing on distance learning and not in bed playing video games. We will all have to learn how to navigate this new reality in the best way possible.

I have been very fortunate to have many advantages after spending years working on a lifestyle that supports my internal and external well-being during times of extreme trial. I have worked from home and attend school online, so I was aware of some of the challenges that were going to come up. These are few things that I have done to keep myself sane and focused during this time.

Every morning I wake up and start the day with prayer, meditation, and Reiki. I have recorded myself saying various prayers and guided meditations. I give myself a full Reiki treatment and send distance Reiki to one of my loved ones. Next, I get up and stretch. This sometimes includes my full yoga practice, though it might just mean I get on my mat and do a few minutes of basic stretching. Then I try to stay outside for a full hour, either going for a walk, run or bike ride. Some mornings I walk or run alone, and others I run with Darelle or walk with Brandy and Beemo. This change of scenery helps me decompress and breaks up the day between my morning routine and work time. Once I'm back home, I take a shower and start my work. Each day is different but most include reading and studying, practicing different exercises, talking to clients and students, grading papers, and writing this book you are reading now. To close out the day, I usually go out to walk or ride my bike for a while. Once I'm home, I take another rinse off and let myself relax.

I give myself the same hour of television that I was allowed as a kid and then it's bedtime. Depending on how tired I am and how the day has gone, I might journal or read before I fall asleep.

My routine works for me. It has been formed over years of digging into the practices that help renew my mind, body, and soul. This is your invitation to find the routines and practices that support you. My clients have done the same, and I have seen amazing things happen in their lives. New jobs, new places to live, new businesses, financial freedom, and internal issues healed. We have been blessed to come through this horrific and historic year better than before. At times I have been shocked and stretched to my limit, but I have remained grateful.

Exercise Nine: Developing A Life You Enjoy

What new skills would you like to learn and incorporate into your day to help renew your mind, body, and soul? Here is a basic self-assessment I give my clients to help find ways they can support their life. It can help you gauge where you are and where you want to go. Use the exercises you have learned in this book to create the life you desire. If you need more help, you can always reach out for a consultation.

Self-Assessment Exercise

There are two rounds of this exercise. The first round is self-reflection to understand where you are right now. Read each question and rate on a scale of 1-7 (1= "Not Me" and 7 = "Yes Me") where you are **now** in the following areas of your life. The second round is about understanding where you want to be. Go back through the questions from one to twenty and rate on a scale of 1-7 (1= "Not Me" and 7 = "Yes Me") **where you would like to be** in these areas.

Mental Emotional Health

1. I have feelings of joy, happiness, and optimism on a daily basis.
2. I experience frequent feelings of depression and anxiety.
3. I experience overwhelming feelings of stress frequently.

Physical Health

4. My exercise habits are consistent (3 or more days per week), effective, and enjoyable.
5. My daily feeling is one full of vitality, well-being, and energy.
6. My nutritional intake is 70% or more healthy fresh food consisting of organic vegetables, fruits, whole grains, high-quality protein, and healthy fats.

Work Health

7. I constantly feel organized, productive, and effective at work.

8. I feel my work presents great challenges for me that help me grow professionally.
9. I have work that I love whether it is my career, side business, or volunteer work.

Relationship Health

10. I spend quality time with friends and family often.
11. I have healthy relationships with friends and family.

Financial Health

12. I am aware of and am satisfied with the ebb and flow of my financial patterns.
13. I have a savings and retirement plan.

Spiritual Health

14. My connection with what I believe in as a higher power helps me to maintain feelings of peace, calm, and contentment on a constant basis.
15. I spend time cultivating my spiritual life.

Environmental Health

16. I am actively aware of and managing the levels of toxicity in my home, car, and work environments.
17. I do my part to create and maintain a healthy environment for the world around me.

Fun/Leisure

18. I have scheduled downtime.
19. I have hobbies that I enjoy.
20. I take vacations every year.

Final Words

Congratulations! You have successfully read through many of the secrets to my success. What I hope you take away from this book is that you are powerful and worth the time, energy, and effort it takes to create the life you desire most. I believe this with my whole heart. I have put this belief to the test for my clients and myself. My life is not perfect, but I have found peace and joy in its imperfections. I have a far more positive way of viewing the twists and turns of my journey, and I am continuously grateful to have this outlook.

Many of my clients have used the exercises and thought processes outlined for you in this book. By making time to develop healthy habits, they have created lives they truly enjoy. They decided to go back to school, start businesses, find the career they now love, develop their dreams and make them a reality. My hope is that you will find success with these practices too. I am praying and cheering for you.

Endnotes

1   Florence Scovel Shinn, "The Game of Life and How to Play It," *The Wisdom of Florence Scovel Shinn*, (Fireside Books, 1989).

2   Brené Brown, *The Hustle for Worthiness*, (3C Press: 2010), DVD.

3   Lauryn Hill, "Doo-Wop (That Thing)," *The Miseducation of Lauryn Hill*, Sony, 1998.

4   Socrates, *Plato's Apology* 38a.

5   Dyer, D. W. (2004). The Power of Intention. Carlsbad, California • New York London • Sydney e Johannesburg Vancouver e Hong Kong • New Delhi, Hay House.

6   *Merriam-Webster*, s.v. "affirmation (n.)," accessed October 21, 2020, https://www.merriam-webster.com/dictionary/affirmation.

7   William Lee Ran, *Usui/Holy Fire® III Reiki Master Manual,* (International Center for Reiki Training 2019).

8   Bluepress, D. b. (2020). "Crown Chakra Affirmation Shower Curtain." from https://www.redbubble.com/i/shower-curtain/Crown-Chakra-Affirmation-by-Bluepress/50358438.YH6LW.

9   *Merriam-Webster*, s.v. "currency (n.)," accessed October 21, 2020, https://www.merriam-webster.com/dictionary/affirmation

10   Dyer, D. W. (2004). The Power of Intention. Carlsbad, California • New York London • Sydney e Johannesburg Vancouver e Hong Kong • New Delhi, Hay House.

11   Florence Scovel Shinn, *The Wisdom of Florence Scovel Shinn*, (Fireside Books, 1989).

12   Florence Scovel Shinn, *The Wisdom of Florence Scovel Shinn*, (Fireside Books, 1989).